In Advance Of All Parting

IN ADVANCE
OF
ALL PARTING

ANSIE BAIRD

WHITE PINE PRESS / BUFFALO, NEW YORK

WHITE PINE PRESS
P.O. Box 236
BUFFALO, NEW YORK 14201

With thanks to the following publications, in which some of the poems first appeared:

The Quarterly: "In a Distant Country," "The Hang-Glider," "New Years Day."
Paris Review: "Long Trek," "Getting There," "What We Have Done,"
"Genealogy," "What She Knows."
Western Humanities Review: "Breathing Lessons."
Denver Quarterly: "Half My Life."
Southern Review: "Housekeeping."
The Recorder: "What Happened Next."

Cover painting: "The Curved Staircase" by Catherine Parker.
Copyright ©2009 by Catherine Parker. Used by gracious permission of the artist.

Publication of this book was made possible, in part, with public funds from the New
York State Council on the Arts, a State Agency.

First Edition.

ISBN: 978-1-935210-09-2

Printed and bound in the United States of America.

Library of Congress Control Number: 2009932981

For my Mother and my Father

and for

Robin Magavern
1935–2009

"Our revels now are ended."
—Shakespeare, *The Tempest*

TABLE OF CONTENTS

PART I

PART II

PART IV

PART V

I

GENEALOGY

Concoct the stories of your own life,
The masks and costumes assumed from infancy.
Make up the true things as well as the lies.
They languish like myths, yours for the using.

Take over ancient history in any way
That suits you. Pluck your authentic ancestors
Out of the smolder of antiquity, those
Glaring flashbacks from your ebullient past.

I, myself, for instance, trace my lineage
On my mother's side directly to the Maid
Of Orleans, her insistent voices leading
To the flames, while somewhat farther back down

The stony road of yore stands my father's
Forebear, Judith, just emerging from
The gaudy tent, the head of Holofernes
Held aloft triumphant in her valiant hand.

And I will not forget the wastrels,
The pick-pockets, the wet-nurses, the
Pioneers, the smudged-faced babies strapped
To the backs of women washing linens.

This vast array of relations remains
The comfort of my old age, brave ancients
And obscure anomalies all intertwined,
All huddled together under the debris

In my attic, descending on the occasional
Quiet evening to enlarge my parlor
With familiar faces I can count on,
Companions when the roof begins to shatter.

LEAVING THE COUNTRY

Where I was born gates closed
And opened on command.
This was called The Field House.

A tall man lay on the parlor floor.
I crawled his length, exploring.

All the couches wore sheets.
At the top of the stairs the head
Of a moose loomed out at me.

We dressed in white to sing
Praise God in the sky.

A rat got in the cage and ate
Poor sad Clare's canary.

Behind The Big House, in a grove of larch,
A stern man sculpted stone busts.
No one called Bill anything but Bill.
He tossed me in the pool, commanding: Swim!
I gasped and Agnes rescued me. Perhaps
My mother and Bill were special friends.
Agnes wept and played the harpsichord.

Even the peonies were extremely pink.
Tiny ants crawled in and out the petals.

Bill ran off with a foreigner from town
Who Lavinia said looked like a coffee table,
Short and squat, perfect
For putting things on.

Leaving home, I held my breath
All the way to the Big Turn.
We passed the graves of ancient hounds:
Beau and Belle and Nemo,
Skipper, Zephyr, Dexter, Dan.

A row of elders arched over the road,
Lush green, flat clusters of lavender,
Bowing us away through private tunnels.

GRIEF IN A FOREIGN TONGUE

My father was a friend of Princess Romanov in Paris, 1949.
I'm not sure how frequently they met.
She was very beautiful, the great niece
of the murdered czar, but what did I care?
Her handsome son Michael smiled at me when
they invited us to their box at the Paris Opera
where Serge Lifar danced Icarus in a white tunic,
leaping and falling as though drowning in the sea.
I couldn't take my eyes off him. I was only eleven but could sense
the strain between my parents, my mother's detached *politesse*
when introduced to the Princess. I wondered
whether I was expected to curtsey, half wished that I were.

Another time we heard *Carmen* with Irina Romanov.
I learned one song by heart
so when I took the long bus rides to my strange new school,
changing at the Etoile while November slush attacked my ankles,
I could hum *"l'amour est enfant de désir."*

All winter we moved from one shabby pension to another.
My mother painted flat white skies and rooftops in her studio.
She rarely introduced us to her friends. My father
wrote at the *Bibliothèque Nationale* or went to tea with royalty.
I knew enough not to ask questions
though they burned in my throat like charred toast.
Where was everyone? Why did the metro smell so desolate?
And that filthy little man who opened his trousers to me
in *deuxième classe*, leaving me stunned into horror and silence.
I counted off the weeks in my *cahier* until we could sail
for home or I could marry Michael Romanov.
Things didn't work out that way. They seldom do.

MARRIAGE A LA MODE

Sauve qui peut
muttered my mother

Tant pis   tant mieux
pondered my father

A tout à l'heure
called my mother
heading out
to meet her lover

Don't bother
replied my father
shutting the front
door after

THE STATUE

My father, the cuckold, the sculpted bust in the garden,
Holds his stone pose, his poise,
Throughout another blast of winter.
Snow mantels his cold shoulders, the slant bones of his face.
His blank oval gaze emerges out of granite,
Overlooking Dwarf Village, abandoned also by mythic creatures,
Only gates and pillars left erect,
Wrecked turrets and cupolas set at odd angles in the landscape,
Railings and doorways rotting or rusting in the high-grown grass
Where they collapsed before some other worlds collapsed.

These wrought iron ornaments, rickety gazebos,
Quaint relics from a ceremonial time,
Remind him of his slap-dash ho-hum love-life gone to seed.
Hunching beneath the weight of weather,
My father stares into the indifferent air, unfazed and frozen.

LOSING THE SPECTRE

My father bows to me and moves away.
He is the shadow lurking on the stair,
The sudden laughter rustling the air.
I seek him in the silence of the day
Which mimics all the silence of the years
We propped him by a window in his chair,
His clenched fist, the fury of his stare
Mute answer to the question of my tears.
Loose-leaf notebooks clutter and obscure
Messages abandoned on a table.
The life he left behind becomes a fable
I memorize, a process to endure
Letting go this figure in disguise.
I see and still I do not see his eyes.

MY MOTHER, NEWLY DIVORCED AT FORTY,
RETURNS FROM WORK TO WORK ON A PAINTING

When she stood at her easel at
The edge of evening
In a city at the edge of Lake Erie,
A glass of rye whiskey teetering
At the edge of the window sill
In the closet she called her studio

But anyone else would call a closet,
At the end of the living room
Where her two lumpy daughters
Slouched or teetered on the edges of
Over-stuffed chairs or the couch,
Twisting and twisting their lank hair,

The room smelling of turpentine and
Linseed oil and Joy, her favorite
French perfume, and a lamb stew
Simmering in the adjacent closet-kitchen
While her palate knife scraped pigment
In devoted gestures to the very edge of
The expansive canvas she was facing,

You might swear she didn't hear
The clamor of sadness tap-tapping
At her casement window, you might
See the vast cathedral beginning
To emerge against a pale Parisian sky,
And she its architect garbed
In her paint-smeared cotton smock,

You might believe she was transporting
Herself stroke by bold stroke
Over the smoky local rooftops of regret,
The pervading ochres and umbers of night,
Edging the sunless corners of her work
With slashes of transforming white.

THE PARTIAL SKULL

After her divorce, my mother
Kept a skull on her mantelpiece

Above the moss brown tiles
And the fake fire in the grate.

Half a skull, really. It was missing
The lower jaw, so it rested

On the bottom of its top jaw,
As if that long angle were its chin.

No nose, or ears. These parts,
And tongue, disintegrate early.

But one spectacular eye gazed out,
Manic and glittery,

Which a madman made
From the top of a Budweiser beer can.

She liked the way it jarred
With the Ming vase

And the quaint ceramic toad
From Aunt Rose.

She kept the thing
For its abandon,

It too having been discarded
With half a life.

THE EARTH IN ITS ORBIT

Aren't you glad we're third from the sun?
my daughter, age five, inquired of my mother.
The child had just mastered the planets, desired
to share her delight in their order with her grandmother,
who, frail and ancient, as I then conceived,
smiled and continued on her way to die.
Nine planets shuddered in their rigid route,
the moons receded, seven oceans gasped,
all oxygen burned out of the blue sky
when flames enveloped my mother's frame,
sending her hurtling through the universe.
And I, already older now than she had ever been,
observe the world's tilt, that which can be seen.
Look, here we are on Earth and the fields are green.

WHAT HAPPENED NEXT

At the lip of Autumn,
the girls had gathered
to see her out.
It was a small room
overlooking the orchard,
white and plain,
ecstatic in clarity.
She said, Lift me up,
open the window wide,
let in the wind.
She was ninety-two,
after all, her three
daughters agreed,
a fine life despite
the sorrows.
I'm ready, she said,
but I don't know how.
Yes, you do,
one replied.
She stroked her mother's
cheek, the others
bent close.
You go first,
their mother begged.
You show me how.
No, they said,
it's your turn now.
We promise
it'll be easy.
Okay, she cried, raising
her arms up to her girls.
Here I go.
Closed her eyes
and seemed to sleep

again, such gallant sleep,
so deep, within an hour
she'd gathered all her days
into the wide circumference of a pond.

WHAT WE HAVE DONE

My mother shrugged off life
Three thousand miles from Paris,
City of her birth. It takes
Two weeks of bureaucratic tape
Before I fly her scant remains
From Buffalo to this historic place,
May 9, 1975, a fine night
For being scattered, if ever
There was one. Co-conspirators,
We creep beneath the Pont Neuf,
My mother and I, she beneath
My coat in a cold container,
And then I dump her in the Seine,
As I promised to do.

How her dozing old bones
Must gape at the ancient stones.
How surely my mother laughs
At what we have done, laughs
To have come home like this,
Laughs and laughs from her sandbar
In the Seine where she lies
Like fragments of an old ghost,
The ashes of a medieval saint,
In the mud of her resting place.

BESIEGED BY ANGELS

I am besieged by angels.
They catch me turning my back
On the wind-washed ashes
Of last Spring,
Spin me around to face again
Dark water running under the bridge,
Tide rising in the river,
In the sea.
These angels speak to me.
They cluster in wheelchairs
Around sliding doors.
Afghans patched in aqua, pink and orange
Cover their laps, their heads
Are covered with fringe. Faces shrink,
Fingers fumble at sleeves.
I bend beside one, calling her name.
What is my name, I say.
What is disturbed from slumber
Speaks to me.
She bows, ferocious and tender, and calls my name:
"Beloved."

THE LONG TREK

I murder my own grandmother   stuff
her corpse in my top bureau drawer
among my underwear   nightmare of
tiny folded body like a lamb's
limp lifeless limbs   eyes closed
but not in sleep   in death among
my underpants   my mother calls to me
from somewhere else   perhaps down-
stairs   perhaps last year before she
disappears and enters my top bureau
drawer among all those vast spaces
in the cellar where she greets my
father hunched beneath the furnace
humming his one tune   *Some Enchanted*
Evening   off-key as usual and some-
thing stirs in the steamer trunk   it is
my only sister   back again and grimy
from the long trek out of the earth

ANTIQUE DESK WITH OPALS, PERHAPS

If you tug at this tiny metal chain
Connected to the empty socket of
The long since eliminated light bulb,

She'll begin to emerge in silver slivers
And reflected fragments from the cubby
Holes and slots and shattered drawers,

The banished panels, secret sliding sections
You can press on gingerly when you're
Running short of cash or searching for

The last divorce decree. Should you
Decide to retrieve those Spanish opals
After all, they might reside just behind

The shredded wedding album, near
Someone's fractured tooth set inside
A gray suede case. If the desk seems to you

A trifle wobbly, if it trembles up and
Down its gilded wooden legs, well
Then, so does Granny who has long

Since evanesced, gone to join the
Debris in the family mausoleum,
Bequeathing you your fair share of

Griefs along with this battered fragile
Beauty you discover tucked in the
Wistful corner of your attic.

HALF MY LIFE

Half my life I've spent
at the Best Western.
Not the best half, either,
these past six nights
waiting for her to rally or expire,
strapped down in her metal bed
just down the road in a hospital
somewhere southwest of Chicago,
the new year snapping at her heels,
a bitch bull terrier, the old
year slinking out the back path
to the trashbin.
And so it was accomplished
that on the eighth day of January
at something after eleven a.m.
Central Standard Time my tired sister
took her final breath, all monitors
went flat, no bells rang.
At Best Western, the telephone flashed
red, a message at the front desk
somewhere southwest of Chicago.
You couldn't come this far
from home for less.

GETTING THERE

Yes, like you, I too have been summoned
by an urgent phone call from someone
whose name I never knew
and I have taken the very next plane
alone to a strange dark city on a January night,
New Year's Day as it happened, and
I too have stood on the concrete island
at the massive airport terminal flagging down
unwilling limousines, all chrome and glass,
and have been driven at last down looping roads,
through unfamiliar towns and neighborhoods
to the wrong entrance of an unfamiliar hospital
where I have walked the long hallways, carrying
my lug-heavy suitcase close to midnight
down unlit passages and into incorrect elevators,
past empty nurses' stations where only the blue
blinking light of some translucent tubing
indicated there was a soul alive and I have entered
swinging doors marked Do Not Enter,
marked Isolation, marked Intensive Care,
and I have arrived alone in my black wool coat,
my suitcase dragging at my shoulder,
and have turned into one small square of light
to find one weary nurse waiting for me there
and she has gently taken my baggage
from my hands and placed it in a safe space
just behind her metal desk and I have shed
my winter coat and scarf and gloves and boots,
placing them in the sterile vestibule,
and donned the sterile paper gown and clumsy
sterile paper covers for my shoes
and I have stuffed my long blonde hair inside
the sterile cap not unlike those motel shower caps
and I have tied a gauze mask up above my nose

and down below my mouth, around my throat,
and like you I have done all this alone and
very late at night, as you have done,
and have stepped in, numb and bewildered,
to the final sterile cell where,
all but unrecognizable, bloated and bald,
my sister lies heaving in her wounded flesh.
And I leaned over her then, finally, tenderly,
and stroked her shaven head and called
to her through all those corridors of pain,
as you have called.
Clare, I have said. Open your eyes, I have said.
Look, I have said. I am here.

BEACH COMBER

Sorrow sits in my pocket
like an old stone.
Sometimes, oh, say once an hour,
I place my hand inside my ample
pocket to rub my thumb
along its gritty surface.
Sometimes it's as slippery as
oil. Another hour it scrapes
where my skin splits in the place
between my several secret fingers.
In due time, I stoop down
and remove it from my shoe
where it rubs my heel raw. How
it migrates there, I'll never know,
slinking into unexpected spots,
with a bit of lint forever attached.
Once in a blue moon, as the song
says, I remove it from my shoe
or pocket just to stare at the mottled
surface where it throbs in my palm.
Its hue is neither aquamarine
nor onyx, more basalt beige or gray,
greasy like the Atlantic on a March
day, insistent as a pebble
indistinguishable from countless
others. Not semi-precious. But
it's mine, so I say it's one in a million,
my hard sorrow, my own stone.

WHAT SHE KNOWS

She finds no list of names to comfort her.
Do not nudge her shoulder and ask
What bird is perching on the branch.
Do not inquire where the oleander blooms.
Nor does she recognize the kinds of clouds.
Of stones or shells. Nature is not her kinsman.

She dreams he appears on latticed porches,
On terracotta roofs of slanting houses.
He is speaking, although he was mute,
Walking, although he was lame,
Flushed and ruddy, although he is dead.
She is certain of nothing except this

And that her husband alters,
A madman who bloats in the dark.
She is able to play the piano not at all.
There is the oak and the common tree,
The rose and the common flower,
The crow and the common bird,
Venus in the sky and all the other stars.

6 A.M. AND ALL IS LOST

My mother lives across the street
In someone's chimney pot.
She died when I was seventeen.
I think of her a lot.

My father is a Spanish duke.
I found him in a book.
He must not speak but now and then
He sends a tender look.

I'm married to a man of snow
Whose eyes are anthracite.
His wooden sign says Caution. Ice
Is building in the night.

I keep a tiny little girl
Who follows me about.
She'll bring me sticky buns to eat
When I am old and stout.

II

STILL-LIFE

Artificial intimacy, also known as talking to each other,
replicates a kind of urgent intimacy, leaving you free to
breathe without the awkward unbuttoning of outer garments,
shedding of clothing better left undisturbed or else everything
escalates into oblivion with its obvious ecstasies and complications.
The still-life gives your life its central stillness, a sort of gravitas,
its serious location viewed from a certain doorway where you rest,
absorbing certain mottled pears beside a crystal goblet placed just
so on a pewter plate you recognize as yours. It's like being naked
with a man, this strip of pear just resting in your hand, brief sweetness
for your parched mouth, silence exactly balancing with speech, an
equal blend of each, of reaching and withdrawal, something resting
always on your tongue, unsavored, like the awful pauses between
stanzas in the song your mother sang as she lathered your sweet body
in the porcelain tub, you so young and tongue-tied. You never knew
whom she was grieving for. Perhaps she was happier than her song.
And the long pauses. Who is the galloping stranger in his crimson coat,
riding his dappled roan across the mottled morning, ascending the same
hill, leaving without waving, who is he? The body knows what it waits
for. The still-life held still. The heart a coffer for such vanished things.

THE QUESTION

Why did the gang of us bother to
bundle up and drive through the dark
over one road after another, and many
of the roads rutted, to arrive finally at
The Observatory and stand packed on
a creaky platform among rapt strangers
listening to the honored astronomer with
the impossible Slavic accent gesturing
upward, one emphatic thrust following
another, undeterred by our total lack of
acquaintance with that expansive spangle,
when instead each of us could amble down
our own paths to the ocean, those celebrity
galaxies right above our heads performing
their flashy acrobatics free of charge,
as they do on summer evenings at the beach,
where, unenlightened as a single star,
we'd linger at the edge of everything,
mute and fixed amid such scattered bliss.

BELIEVE IT

My friend from St. Paul
Drove all the way to
St. Louis to see the sun
Eclipse the moon or
The moon eclipse the sun
I forget which one.

Oblivious, I switched on
The electric light and
Kept on writing while
Midday slouched aside
And my desk shrouded itself
In sudden dusk.

My specific sun reigns
Right where it always does
If I happen to glance up
And that cool slippery
Moon stays casually slapped
Flat against black.

No doubt each orb cuts
Loose from time to time
When I'm not checking.
Good luck to them. Good
Luck to all of us
Who flail and spin

In transitory light
But stay the course.

AND ALL OF US ALIVE

So there we were and all of us alive,
Embracing on the Atlantic beach
Near midnight, Nantucket time in breezy May,
While the moon went through its paces
Of flash and dazzle and farewell
And the stars skimmed by on their
Oblivious errands through outer space,
Disinclined to stay in place so we five
Could trace their outlines into ancient
Constellations as the Greeks could.

Sure, we'd had plenty of fine wine,
Or anyway ample to the occasion.
One of us said, Let's go down to the shore
And we did and stood there amazed,
Gazing as though we'd never seen it all before,
This panorama, this flamboyant sky,
And one of us about to die
Although we couldn't say for sure which one or why.

So off we laughed and stumbled on the path,
Dipped and danced and strutted on the sand,
Grabbed hands and held each other in our arms
While the sea clamored and the winds churned
And we sang our mortal hearts out to the moon.

TAKE A RIGHT TURN AT ONEIDA

FOR HAYDEN CARRUTH

Any day now I'll be heading out North
To visit the old man of Munnsville,
Carting along supper and two or three bottles
Of booze which we'll imbibe while I soak up
All his lunacy and wisdom,
Wrestled from eighty-six fretful years upon this planet.

The guy resembles a sort of Old Testament prophet,
Disheveled hair, scruffy beard resting on his chest.
Only the translucent plastic tubing jutting from his nose
And a tank trailing along from bed to desk to ancient kitchen chair
Betray his up-to-date condition, or, as he'd say, over-the-hill,
About-to-croak.

Meanwhile he sends me up-to-date indignant letters berating me
For sticking with the same old subjects:
For crissakes, forget about that bastard.
You're wasting time yearning for the past.
There's plenty to write about just outside your window:
Glint of ice on the downed power line;
Your spotted dog circling the swings.
You know as well as I do how the Earth exhales in beauty.

I write him back: You're right, of course,
Old pal, old microphone,
Ranting at the world's injustices
And all the dreck we find in poetry.
You never stray from telling me the truth.
Keep holding on. I cherish you for that.
When your forsythia blooms, I'm coming back.

MARCH PILGRIMAGE

Behold the ashen cat poised
On the kitchen counter.

Behold the old man at the stove,
Boiling up a cup of ginger tea.

His hands tremble, his stained
Beard drips like egg on his chest.

Behold his lush young wife, bent double
In pain. Her liver's wracked.

Her scarlet Chinese jacket shot with
Black dragons gapes over her white nightie.

Behold the hospital bed amid the crumpled parlor.
They take turns taking naps. The tv mutters on.

It's Spring in Munnsville but it isn't Spring.
Everywhere is mud and melting snow.

Some valiant buds threaten to erupt
Beside the battered fence. Not yet. Not yet.

The feeble-minded woman from next door reports
She's seen a robin but it isn't so.

You've arrived with soup and bread,
Lemon cake and lilies from a long way.

No wine. No way. No longer
It's permitted in this place.

The spasm past, the young wife straightens up,
Cuts a slice of cake for each of you.

Quite stealthily the pain slinks in again
To grin and slice her into disarray.

He bends to take her in his frail embrace,
Her auburn hair a flair against his chest.

Civility prevails and ancient love.
You gulp your soggy tea and settle in to stay.

THE MAIN ATTRACTION

The talking statue strides up and down
The corridors of the museum. He strides
In and out the swinging doors of the museum,
Up and down the wide marble staircase,
His corrugated steel feet resounding on stone.

He descends to the basement and fools around
With the generators. He makes steam heat
Surge out of the radiators with a wild whoosh
Or he switches off the blower altogether so a
Frigid wind gusts over the folks upstairs.

The talking statue struts into the surrounding
Park. Sometimes he disappears among the trees
And shrubbery for weeks. More frequently
His clunk-clank or his stomp-stamp footfall
Can be made out over the sound of bird song

If you've a mind to listen. He's a big money-
Maker for the museum. People pay cash to catch
A glance of him. He'll stand and prance or else
He bows and tips his cap, a courtly stance, then
Winks a wicked eye and grimaces wildly.

Or he clams up, says nary a word, not so much
As a chuckle for hours on end. He's unpredictable.
The curators don't know how to market him,
How to publicize his presence because he might be
Absent any time. That's the fun of it, they guess.

He's a real phenomenon, an assemblage of
Bone and string and metal rods and glue and
Rivets and screws and slats and ladders and
Light bulbs and tin cans and rope and raffia
And often he dons real clothes, a different

Outfit for every occasion. Only he always looks
The same whatever he wears, appalling or somewhat
Appealing. In any case there is nothing remotely
Like him in the whole museum so he's definitely
The main attraction. That has to count for something.

BONNARD'S WIFE SPEAKS

It isn't that easy being your wife.
You think I like lying around in
interminable bathtubs while the water
turns tepid, the drain clogs, I try dozing
as the scruffy little dog yaps
throughout the afternoon? And you
sketch on and on and on, oblivious.

Meanwhile those other women lurk always
at the edge of doorways or window frames,
gazing away from me, don't get me started.
You introduce us over café au lait
but they turn their ample backs in silence,
assuming I'm invisible, a sort of
intruder they refuse to recognize.

I'm going to confess something else.
Lavender skin? I mean, you know
perfectly well which tubes of paint
contain flesh tones, the ochers and umbers,
pale beiges and translucent peach. But no,
you go ahead and make my skin glow
violet or puce as inspiration strikes you.

I do the best I can with lotions but god knows
I'm not getting any younger. My sallow body
begins to sag in certain curious places, my
skin to shrivel and hang loose on my frame.
It must be all this time I've spent immersed
in tubs, indulging your view of me as some
sort of water sprite who revels in the damp.

The truth is, I've been longing for dry land,
an invitation to slake my thirsty days within
your vivid arms. There I'd be spritely indeed!
We'd paint the bedclothes every lurid
color in the spectrum: bolts of scarlet,
tangerine and gold. I keep suggesting this
but you insist I have to hold my pose

While you depict me floating in a trance
within the rigid confines of the tub,
a trapped beast wallowing amid the steam
on tiny speckled feet. You think
I don't know everything about your
golden girl? You think I do not churn
and shiver in this hot flush of pink?

My skin glows mottled in its quilt of hues,
Its vivid blues and greens.
The patchwork floor slopes forward
over space, transformed into tapestries
of light. And I lie bathed in purple
like a corpse, my coffined limbs
encased and glazed in shade.

I see your face reflected in the glass
above the porcelain sink, observing me
in all my amplitude. Duplicity, indeed,
to paint your naked wife while craving
someone else. Go ahead, embellish
my flesh with segments of absurd pastels
to keep me from escaping. Wretched love,

I clamber from the bath, a phantom wife
all absence in your view. You may
as well have hung me on the wall,
abandoned effigy within a frame.
Light from my undraped limbs spills
like water on the floor, a pool of blue,
an aureate, a scattering of gold.

UNFRAMED, LIKE LACE

People keep disappearing
into white space,
a pencil sketch,
thin line, a perfect
outline of a body
on the page.
First a foot, a leg
gets erased. Next
the hips are smudged
and then the chest—
only an arm or hand
still clings to the sheet.
Perhaps the hand
is raised, waving.
The head goes last,
the face still
tilting toward you.

Then it, too, is gone
and all you have on hand
is just the trace,
a speck of something gray
once engraved on paper.

Someone gives you an
unframed drawing titled
"Lace: A decorative material
most of which is not there."
But what's left out is
just as clear
as what's left in.
Mystical, maybe; maybe
fragile as the body
on the page

which shreds in tatters
in a matter of minutes.
Useless to try pinning
down the meaning,
pinning up the sketch.

THE CONSOLATION OF THE TABLETOP

after an exhibition of the works of Giorgio Morandi

These cylinders, bowls, basins, empty
vases are set in place against the beige
and gray of fading afternoon. Snug
pots and jugs, platters, jars and dusty
biscuit tins shimmer in radiance, their
skinny ovals and flat globes thrust up
against each other, hunched and nudging
clusters, propped like widows in disguise.
Or perhaps sentinels, stiff columnar
pitchers arrayed to resist an invasion.

The merest hint of blue, a hovering wash,
shivers above taupe stones
and ochre tablecloths, folded with edges
trembling into stillness. More than
absence of sound, here is presence of
clamor gone soft, burnt umber in its mantle
of mourning. No keening. No exclamations
of rage. Rather a sort of disturbing resignation
squabbling for space, serene and turbulent.

And when the visitor exits, he must feel
somehow somewhat compassionate, becalmed,
having glimpsed this throng of noble shapes.

III

NEW YEAR'S DAY

They met again at the street where the heart resides.
Rue Gît Le Coeur, near the butcher of small birds,
Near the stalls where rabbits hang head down
In delicate fur coats, near the ice beds
Where giant fish glitter and stare from their impassive eyes.
They met in a small dive, la Grenouille, green and lively
Like a leaping frog, but they did not dance,
They did not order frog. He arrived
In his brown waterproof coat, hood up,
Although it never rained that week in Paris
And no other man covered his head.
Perhaps he was a monk disguised as her husband.
Perhaps he was her husband disguised as a stranger.
It is the start of a new decade, he said.
I'll be going away, he said. This is no kind of life.
What could she reply? She keeps a fierce cat
Concealed beneath her cape. It claws at her flesh.
Bite by bite it eats her alive.

BUT THAT WAS IN
ANOTHER COUNTRY AND BESIDES

She remembers raising an urgent hand and waving,
waving at a person in the distance who wore a green
winter jacket and was striding through the Tuilleries,
whom she'd just spotted as she stood at her fourth
floor glass doors which opened onto an elegant wrought
iron porch, no not a porch, just a balcony no larger
than one foot deep but still she could lean on its railing
and imagine all of Paris at her feet, the spires and
rooftops and giant ferris-wheel in the park and she
could just barely detect in the breeze the dank familiar
scent of the metro from the stop directly opposite,
but all she really focused on was the man becoming
larger and now larger still as he strode confidently
up the graveled paths, a newspaper tucked under his arm,
his face so handsome she had to gasp and try hard
to resist yelling out Hi! Hey! Up here! making a fool
of herself and infuriating him as he approached and then
disappeared into the lobby of the hotel they always
stayed in together, so that any minute he would
reenter their room, toss his jacket on the nearest
chair and ask, if she was lucky, What have you
been up to while I was gone? But he never did.

A GOTHIC STORY

We were seated in the sun-glutted square
in Strasbourg. He was delighted with
the local hard cider. I ordered a hard cider,
too. I wanted to do whatever he wanted to do.
We'd just come from the cathedral, majestic,
dim and gothic. The sunlight dazzled him.
And then we walked by the canal and ate
choucroute garnie and drank the local beer
at the timbered restaurant with white stucco
walls and a waitress in a quaint lace cap.
It seemed we must be glad to be together.
I thought we loved one another once more
and had come to Strasbourg so we could
take the train to Colmar and spend hours
gazing at the Issenheim altarpiece, this work
of art I long had longed to see, saints and angels
cast in lamentation, ravens gnawing at gobbets
of transcendent flesh, flames radiantly ascending.
How generous of him to come because of me.
How little I knew about his gothic life.
How back at home his lover of the past
two decades waited on in her own isolation
for his erratic chance to take her in his arms.
And some day all of us are going to die.

THE JESTER'S TALE

I'm about at my wits' end
the jester said
I've hummed silly tunes
my entire repertoire
I've strummed my lyre
till my fingers bled
and my throat went dry
I've stood on my head
to regard the stars
and invoke the moon
to help you sleep
but whatever I try
my jokes seem tired
and provide no cheer
or scant relief
I'm doing my best
for you, my friend
but you disappear
where the story ends
and on the last page here's who is left:
the queen of grief, the king of no regret

THE INVISIBLE WOMAN

This here woman who arrived
behind you
who is not here
hangs out on every street corner
sprawls on the bench at the bus stop
she's the woman behind the counter
and the one in the dentist's office
and the one who refuses to let you
exit the car wash and the one who
urges you to get the hell out she
sells you a stamp she sells you a pass
she hangs up the phone when nobody's
there she mows her own lawn
she rues the day she ever let your
fancy man get away and she's on the
come-back trail her Chevy hatch-back
even now pointed in your direction.

HANDIWORK

I wish I could teach you something
about isolation but you have already
mastered the craft, stitched yourself
into a patchwork suit of separation
that seems to fit just right.

I wish you could teach me something
about grief, this great black hawk
circling over my left shoulder,
its insistent caws a collation of phrases
familiar as ordinary speech.

I am not a tailor by trade and you
are not an ornithologist.
Your garb, my bird. Our separate arts.

MISNOMER

This cannot be a tree
although it grows so tall.
It must be something else,
all green to offer shade
and be so tall. What
shall we call it? It is
not a tree.

This cannot be a crime
because it is so deft.
Before you blink an eye
it disappears. What
shall we call it? It is
not a theft.

If you peel back the shingles
of the sky, its wide black roofline,
you'll find they might be only
gaseous balls of luminosity, those
things that we call stars.

In spite of it...
in spite of it
we call them stars.

When you select a name for something new,
you give yourself a chance to make it yours.

So how would you define this mottled state?
It needs another phrase. What
works for you? Would carnage do?
When you contrive another name,
let me know. I'll
write it down.

AFTERIMAGE

I

Stand over here beneath this
flowering branch or maybe here
overlooking the rushing stream.
Place your arm around her shoulder, there,
just so, and pose for the photographer.
A wide smile. Come on. Move in closer.
It's your son's graduation day
or your daughter's wedding day
or the naming day of another baby.
It's hiking in Tuscany in Autumn
or the beach at Wauwinet in sunswept August.
Here's the two of you looking solemn.
It's the day you buried your sister.
And every picture contains a vague taint,
an invisible image gazing over your shoulder,
the ghost in the photograph,
ever present in her abiding absence.
The one you kept turning back to.
You might as well tear these photos
into tiny shreds. Try to envision
something else that might be true.

II

It wasn't all smoke and
mirrors anyway.
The truth is truth
is elusive, lost
in tilted reflections
or shadows cast
on a scrim of silence.

Get real. You are grieving
for what was never there.
An artifice.
An alabaster pear.

SNOW GLOBE

Two small plaster people stand back to back,
each facing away from the other, man and
wife inside a glass globe made with snow
one can shake to make fake crystals
scatter all over their shoulders and their feet.

It is really rather sweet, this standing there
withstanding ice and frost and summer's
heat and whatnot, poised just so inside
their artful globe of painted snow. Until
time warps the plastic base and he escapes,

smashing with tiny fists the glass into great
jagged shards while he prances his way down
the living room, into the front hall, all the way
to the forbidden forest and another's castle.
Her feet, alas, are more securely enmeshed

in the glued-on grass beside a tree inside
the fragile globe. Try as she might, flailing
about and even emitting tiny shouts for
rescue, she never can emerge from behind
the cracked glass bubble placed on the mantel,

shedding artificial snow upon her breast.
It's obvious she's not a pretty sight,
alone at last within the broken glass.

DEBRIS ON THE BEACH

When it washed up on shore
amid the scum of the retreating tide
and lodged against a log in the cove
just at the edge of her path to the bay,
she peered inside the sealed
glass bottle and could see
a folded note, plain as day,
white and dry against the mottled gray.

Naturally she knew the note was launched
from his own isolated island
to be discovered by his castaway
cabin-mate, imploring her to rescue him and
return him to some semblance of civilization.

Prying off the cork with glee,
she poked out the paper with a forked stick
jutting beside her in the sand.
Such joy to see his hand
writing again after all this time!
Ahoy! he wrote. *This is just to say
I've never been happier. Don't try to find me.*

THE STRIPPED BRANCH

She thinks of the old woman
in the Williams poem
who moans
I can't die. I can't die.
Pleading.
And she picks at her own
chapped hands, dry,
unbleeding.
Asks in a flat tone,
Why is it, dear god,
why
is it I can't cry?

THE INSOMNIAC

He used to inhabit the bed
     adjacent to hers.
He was up and down, in and out
     all night long.
She lay awake next to him, wondering
     what in hell is going on.
When he packed his bag and disappeared
     for brief or lengthy spells,
He still continued to sleep in her closet,
     curled up under
The motley mass of clothes he left behind.
     She could hear him
Rustling through the long hard hours
     while she tossed
And turned and then, from time to time,
     turned on the light
To check if he'd returned unexpectedly.
     Sometimes he snoozed
Beneath her bed, muttering in his sleep
     someone else's name.
She lay very still and prayed he'd slip out
     the side door before
Dawn arrived on little cat feet. Then
     one day without warning,
He filled the trunk of his car with foreign cash
     and his outlandish shoes
And drove out the driveway of her life forever.
     She put extra blankets
On her bed and slept and slept like a wild animal
     burrowed deep in its secret lair.
She could scarcely awaken with the alarm clock
     after all this time in the dark.

REMEDY FOR WRECKAGE

If you cannot fix the marriage, fix the face.
Try surgery for lids and chin and neck
When he has vanished, leaving not a trace.

It won't be long that you are feeling ill
And bruised and battered from the outside in.
That's better than the inside out. The skin

Heals faster than the heart. A month at most
Before you leave your bandages and boast
That all you have to suffer is the bill

And suddenly you're rendered young again,
Without your wrinkles and your droopy smile.
Although some call your vanity a sin,

The mirror satisfies and for a while
You manage to believe you're not a freak.
It isn't only beauty that you seek,

But if he's fled with one you've never met,
And you can purchase solace with a check
So you no longer yearn for his embrace,
Then leave the marriage shattered, fix the face.

IN TOUCH

I like being frisked at the airport.
Where else can I ever get touched?
A pat on the side of my pant leg,
A caress that would make others blush.
What's this? Oh, an under-wire garment.
What's that? Oh, a pocket-size pen.
Whenever I exit security,
I wish I could do it again.

I like when I go to the dentist,
Where others would flinch with alarm
As he hovers to drill something desperate
And somehow he brushes my arm.
And his casual touch on my shoulder
Or his fingers aside of my face
While he excavates rot in a molar
Is comfort I cannot replace.

There are seldom sufficient occasions.
There is never enough skin-to-skin.
I'll take any paltry replacements
For my loss, losing him.

NOTHING OF YOU

I

Sometimes I pretend you have tumbled
off the edge of the Persian Gulf,
dropped like a pearl
to the bottom of the sea.

You glimmer but the indifferent fish
swim on.

You are my exotic, my precious
non-possession.

I would have you hammered
into sheets of gold,
molded into a brooch
I could pin on my lapel.

See, I'd say. There he is.
Doesn't he shine?

II

Who's to say?
It may be all
for the best
this fall-
ing off
this dis-
sonance.

Still, when I
stumble
in the pitch
and tremble
of night's pit
            clamor
            clamor
            clamor
shakes me
awake

your name
engraved
in water
on my palm.

DESIRE (TERRYCLOTH)

This is your old bath-
robe giving off heat-

shivers where you
tossed it on the floor

you don't wear
bathrobes, you

inhabit them. You
haunt the fabric

and it glows or
struggles from my

hands. I hang it
up to locate you

against the back
of the bathroom

door you walked
out of only

moments before
already the room

swims in your absence.

THEATER OF THE ABSURD

Anything can happen every day. Today,
for instance, she's acting in a third-rate
docu-drama set in an ordinary musty courtroom,
saved for events less ominous than butchery.
A judge, two lawyers, one court stenographer
and plaintiff (that is she). She's placed before
a stand set with a Bible and a microphone,
dressed in what she presumes is proper
courtroom attire, having no experience in same,
namely a knee-length skirt her mother would
approve. The plaintiff reckons court is like
a funeral and everyone knows you don't
wear pants to attend a funeral.
No longer young, she assumes
a high neckline to hide her wrinkled throat.
But her hand upon the Bible gives her away.

This is just like acting in a play.
Any moment Edward G. Robinson will enter
stage left. Instead the present characters arise
when the judge raises his gavel and proclaims
the court is in session. Proceedings will begin.
The two attorneys, elderly themselves, act
deferential to the presiding figure cloaked
in his robes of black authority. She thinks
her part must still be in rehearsal.
Perhaps it's more like being in a movie.
She spies the plaintiff, overhears her testimony
from an obscure spot atop the Venetian blind.
That is called a long shot. She looks fine.

All her life she's been avoiding this precise
event. All her tumultuous entire life.
So when the gavel bangs again to signify
the hearing is concluded, her divorce is final,
she waits expectantly for the credits to unroll.

THE PROPPED GATE

I thought I was chasing a dying man
But he turned out to be a stranger.

                Danger
Said the sign at the highway's side.
Falling rubble.
Excavations taking place.

                Prepare
For pot-holes, ruts, frozen pits.
Unstable land underfoot. Also

Escaping strangers, thought to be
                Familiar,
Exuding duplicity.
Charlatans cheating at darts.

Stepping gingerly around
Crevasses, I pin a note
To the propped gate:
                I can wait.

PALLBEARER

I carry your corpse
around with me

strapped to my back
some days I nearly

forget you are there
so familiar you are

my spine shaped
to your slack embrace

your dangling arms
at my waist

even the stench
of fetid flesh

is what I expect
after all these days

of lugging the body
funny   what staggers

me is you   still
very much alive

a mile or two
away

your quick silence
my dead weight.

THE ROBE

Grief is the good garment
you carry on your shoulders,
familiar and somewhat cozy.
You own it.

Toss it on the bathroom hook.
It comes in handy as you arise
from a steamy immersion.
With no one home to keep you warm,
it fits just fine.

THE HUNT

It's easy to underestimate
The screech-owl or the
Field mouse or the bat,
Difficult to identify
Their outline in the dark
Woods, their appearance in
The apparently empty barn.

They creep or burrow, flap
And scuttle or remain still.
You may search the attic or
The shack on blue stilts in
The notch of the hill or the
Thicket where creatures
Whistle a plaintive air.

Not much chance to capture
Your prey the conventional
Way, traps or nets or lines
Or speckled lures. Perhaps
You don't yearn to capture
Anything at all except for
The elusive man who leaves

By every possible exit.
How can you hope to
Snare him, recognize
His markings, learn his
Diurnal ways, at home as he is
With the screech-owl or
The field mouse or the bat?

THE PLAYERS

If there had been curtains provided for parting,
Ornate ones, brocade, that swayed amid pleats
On big brass hoops looping everything together,
The finale might have appeared different. Of course
It wouldn't have been different, but facade counts for a lot.

There could have been a leisurely opening scene, followed
By development, transitions, minor characters thrust forward
To explain away one more absence or obscenity,
Distracting the non-existent, disembodied audience
From overhearing two tense voices, relentless dialogue
Interrupted intermittently by soliloquies or silence.

As it was, performed in the round, sans entr'acte,
Not even an intermission to provide some breathing space
Or needed contemplation, the actors made no sense
Of their scripts, often missed cues, failed to explain away
Limitless improbabilities, acquiescences, dubious inventions.

It was bleak out there without scenery to embellish
The repetitious sets. If only those curtains had been set
In place in advance, an actor might have exited decorously,
Speaking in hushed tones. Instead the lead strode out loudly
Down the center aisle and right into the present day
While his opposite fled backstage, makeup caking,
Costume in disarray, plenty of last lines left unsaid.

Epilogue

Years pass. Long past,
The director recognizes why
It had all gone dreadfully wrong, the principals entirely
Miscast. No wonder.
No wonder listeners were baffled by conflicting texts.
Save the Playbill if you must.
Paste it away, a curiosity from an ancient failure.

LEGACY

Someday when we are dead
or maybe senile,
you'll write the murky fable
of our lives:
how one of us turned up
in seamy places
and one of us stalked shadows
in the cloisters
and one of us prattled
to the creatures
and one of us held battles
with the bottle
and one of us hid bottles
by the boat house
and both of us drank venom
with our coffee
and bandaged open sores with
antic laughter
and brandished scissors or
a Spanish onion
till real tears ran down our real cheeks.
It won't be fun but you'll
write the story.
You'll find the stuff packed
in motley boxes.
It's just a matter then of
how to sort it out.

IV

FACTS OF THE MATTER

What manner of matter is packed into boxes
The clatter of insights
The shatter of daylight
The silence of years as they slip into cupboards
Or stumble in clusters
Or mumble in echoes
The blur of the page yielding tomorrow
The cobweb of joy swindled by sorrow
The parcels, the packets, the folded, the faded
The early, the only, the stolen, the traded
The cartons, the contents, the attic, the basement
All scattered and lonely, no matter the placement
We gather the matter
To last when we perish
We bundle it roughly
And strew what we cherish.

THE COMPLETE DEVELOPMENT OF GREEN

Some restaurateurs think they know everything.
You order the foie gras, they bring plates of baked beans.
Better for whatever ails you, they proclaim.

Some music mavens think they know everything.
You request string quartets, they're convinced you desire
To mellow out on Gumbo Rock. Oh yeah!

Some travel agents think they know everything.
You yearn for Venice in verdant Spring, they produce
Albania in August, rife with rutted roofs and fissures.

Some men think they know everything.
You ask for answers, their silence shatters stained
Glass, their smirks press shards in your skin.

So you are making your way towards
Perfection over a snowy field when,
Without warning, everything begins
Turning green. Oh, great, you say,
Green is taking over the universe.
Blooming green, serene green, soft
Silver and insistent green. You move
Into it grudgingly, only to find yourself
Clad in the deep radiance of new leaves.

NIGHT WATCH

Seven dark hawks
inhabit my head
pernicious birds
talons embedded
in gray matter
no matter
uninvited
they flap back
in for a landing
their clatter
keeps me awake
for their sake
I recite the
night long
lists of all my
indiscretions
they peck & caw
implacable
seven sins
of my relentless
history   their
nightly arrival
a voracious
invasion   some
sort of dread
penance   these
feasters on
succulent tidbits
these spectral
companions   this
kind of relief.

THE UNDERSIDE OF THE WORLD

Don't die in China,
my son says,
leaning against me at the front door
as he leaves for school,
his Bison baseball cap askew.
He's off to the corner yellow bus,
I to the underside of the world—
Beijing, Nanjing—
who knows where?
My suitcases, two sentinels,
guard the sacred doorway.
Please don't go, he mumbles.
But I must. Plans set in motion
lifetimes ago lead me inexorably
to the Lung of the Cow Gorge,
the Dipping Dragon Cavern,
the Fragrant Stream of the Forgotten Princess.
Good-bye. Good-bye. The child
grabs his sack of books,
makes a dash for it.

IN A DISTANT COUNTRY

Navigating the Three Gorges of the Yangtse
takes all his concentration
so Captain Chao Wen does not smile for three days.
My gray-faced guide gives me names
for everything: This is the seaslug soup, this
is the Peak of the Wounded Stork, this
is the Dark Cave of the Unlucky Brother.
This is the man you will not see again.
Look, here is the rock named Coming Toward Me.
It may be true, he says, it whines
and whistles, beckoning.
The Captain pays it no mind.
The mind is a rock named
coming toward me.
It lodges here, in my swift currents.
If I should reach to grip its jagged edges,
it will slit my fingers,
spill my blood into the humming river.

A CHINESE TOUR AMONG STRANGERS

We rubbed raw silk through our fingers,
bought rugs newly woven in rich aqua,
weighed hunks of jade in our hands,
debating the color, the date.
Our guide was kind. He said:
"Now, friends, here is a pagoda nine stories high.
From its top you may see patterns
of plowing the rich countryside.
Now, friends, please be back at the bus by two-fifteen."

Why did we buy and buy,
amassing antique rosewood boxes,
lacquered plates, six inlaid jewel cases
to lug home? My ivory water buffalo,
your amber and gold beads?

At night the Yangtse flashed lights
as we danced to Perry Como.
Chopsticks became light in our deft fingers.
Your hands shuffled the cards too fast,
making me laugh as you cheated at gin.
I was light as leaves
when I crept down unfamiliar hallways,
back to my ordinary bunk
with its extraordinary silk comforter.

And fast as shutters click, the trip was over,
you to Hong Kong to buy the perfect pearls,
I back across the Pacific, wakeful and silent.

These things circle and merge
like the whorls I try to count
on the umbrella of the tiny man
who leans forward, ancient and serene,
on the back of the carved water buffalo
I bought for too much money in Chongging.

THE HANG-GLIDER

I

FROM AN ALBUM, INCOMPLETE

Here's the earliest, black and white.
You bend over your small son and your wife
Smiles straight out at me.

At the airport we strike a formal pose,
Your arm around my shoulder like an owner.
I'm in my same old departure dress.

I ask you for a picture by the pond.
Lazy, sated, sun in your face,
You sprawl, a big lug.

But back on the tractor, masterful,
You and the ancient machine engage
In slaughter with the underbrush.

Or stalking the high night meadow
Under the moon, an orange paste-up,
You find a new view for ploughing.

Sometimes, playing Icarus,
You sail from sand dunes over the ocean,
Grinning under gold and purple wings.

When you test stiff winds,
Flouting the mist,
I think I'll never see you again.

II
CAPE KIAWANDA, AT THE COAST

Often in late September light
You clambered hand over hand
Up the steep bluff

Lured by the urgent promise of the sky.
And it was like wings!
Brave painted silk all bold

And purple in the cold autumn air.
Stripes flapped you into action,
The glider struggling to launch itself
Out over sullen water.
What to do, after all,
With so much sky and water

But to pitch out & up & over
And try, with wild extravagance, to fly.
Then the bright wings failed.

At dusk, on a cliff by the Pacific,
You fell, face-down into colors
Crumpled like the strings of silk

Magicians pluck from their sleeves.
And died, amazed,
While strangers pounded your chest

And a clumsy truck lurched down the beach
To fetch your sweet body back
And burn you into ashes.

BREATHING LESSONS

Because you refuse to give me
directions for anything except
how to breathe, I try to relax and
breathe exactly the way you
tell me to. Sometimes it works.
It actually does sometimes work.
I breathe in and out sometimes
for an entire afternoon. I imagine
I am the Queen of Spain and
you are the Prime Minister, my
breathing instructor, my interpreter
at The Court of Royal Surprises. How
did you learn to achieve such fluency?

I knew a man once who forever
held his breath right in the middle of
significant moments. Without
notice, he would disappear, flatten out,
slip into the mirror, turn himself
inside out, invisible. He never did
acquire the knack of easy breathing,
just in and out, in and out, like a
squeeze box, lungs expanding and
contracting in tune to the music, an
unheard melody, one of those sweet ones.
Today, again, I intend to begin breathing.
Tomorrow I might actually break into song.

KEEPING TRACK

Dear one, there is a pandemonium
        in my brain.
Small men in sarongs rush up and
        down stone temple steps
        beating brass gongs.

From the far hills I can overhear
        the squawking of birds,
        perhaps peacocks or
        the arresting rooster.

With you not here confusion
        mocks their calls.

Is it Winter on the train to Vladivostok?
        You may be reading this by lamp-
        light if there is overhead light
        in your compartment
        and if the filament endures.

No doubt you've concealed a biscuit
        in the pants pocket
        of your second best suit.
        Chew on it.

IN ADVANCE OF ALL PARTING

In those days I used to love Monday,
knowing I would see you again on
Tuesday, since most weeks Monday
comes the day before Tuesday, meaning
most weeks I'd see you the next day and
so Mondays were my second favorite day
of the week, in those days when I used to
love Monday. But lately I've begun to dread
Monday because it means I'm only a little over
twenty-four hours away from not seeing you
again after I've just seen you and as long
as it's a few days until I see you again,
I won't have to say goodbye to you soon again.
Yet now it seems as if Tuesday is here before
Monday is half over and then it's Wednesday
before I've even begun to cherish Tuesday
and sometimes Tuesday disappears into
actual absence and those actualities are so
inconceivable that I'm longing in advance
for it to be the previous Sunday so that Monday
might be the day after Sunday and Tuesday
would rest in the foreseeable future, almost
present but not so near as to be about to be
absent, in those days when I used to love Monday.

IN THIS OTHER ALBUM

I am looking at a picture
        of your wife.
I am looking at you
        looking at a
picture of your wife.
        I am looking at
the picture of you with
        your hand
around the small shoulder
        of your wife.
I am looking up from looking
        at the picture
of your wife and here you are
        looking right at
me handing me a picture
        of yourself
snapped when you were far
        away from me
even though you're far
        away from me
sometimes when you're sitting
        close to me.
It makes me feel close
        to you to
look together at this picture
        of your wife.
Thank you for the picture
        of your wife.
Finally now I picture what
        she looks like.
She looks nice.
        Your wife.

THE PRAIRIE

Some days I believe I can live
without you.
Ice on the river forms late
this year.
Lake effect storms still batter
the city
way into January. It helps to have
cleats on
sturdy boots for going outside.
Most do.
My feet slide, I lose my grip
on things.
The sidewalk, you, are moving out
of reach.
An accumulation of plowed snow,
an eyesore,
towers at the corner, the way out
gritty, icy.
Winter is long and bitter cold,
my heart.
Only the sissies complain in
this town.
Mute members of a steel herd,
cars hunch
and shudder their shaggy way along
clogged avenues,
rutted like the ancient prairie.
Strange beasts,
people struggle or huddle against
the wind,
their silent mouths entirely covered
with scarves.
You can barely discover their eyes.
Bare-headed,

I walk out into the morning storm,
seeking to
catch perhaps a glimpse of you
passing by.

If I see you it means
one thing.
If I don't see you it
means another.
It means I am going
to die.
I never see you anywhere.
Wrong again.
See, I am still alive here
in Buffalo.

THE NECESSARY GESTURE

Hold out your hand
here just
begin to bend
forward or
attempt to
hand it over
quick don't
let it slip
through your
fingers your
fingertips just
grazing just
barely touching
grip the wrist
across the void
hard to hang
on to it
hand to hand
combat comes
to mind but
doesn't come
in handy
here stroke
caress or
press gently
oh yeah press
this flesh
grasp it
a bit more
give it a
firm shake
at least make
sure you
seem to

connect
more just
here just
reach out your...
hold onto my
extended hand.

THE STING OF IT

If I cared about such things
I'd write you the wild
daffodils are blooming
and crocuses and ye gods
blue hyacinths and a clutch
of coral tulips at the curb.
And you not here
and I disinclined
to care about such things,
about Spring, your absence
a wasp entangled in my hair.

ALMOST A PAVAN

Frequently they are called upon to perform
The Shoulder Rub, an ancient Celtic dance
Practiced by partners who do not move much,
Preserve a stately style, barely even glance
At one another. She is required to fix her eyes
On the spare square of space they occupy,
While he must seem to be gazing out
Over her head at an unseen panorama,

Some floating rooftops tucked in smoky hills
Where peat bogs burn out the evening.
Their feet advance in measured motion,
One of four knees lifts while the other three
Dip and they keep their backs stiff, turn aside
Their heads, seem only by circumstance
To nudge against each other, an accident or
Chance amidst the formal progress of the dance.

The culmination appears to be a subtle touch
By each along the other's upper arm, something
Less than a stroke, more than a brush of air,
An element of ritual, you could say.
In any case, they've perfected the gesture.
Now they move apart, the last action of
The Shoulder Rub, an ancient Celtic dance of separation.
It happens so fast, the music can't keep up.

WANTED

Wasn't it perfect irony, my dear,
My letters went astray, were
Undelivered, left lying in disarray
On a weathered desk in the second best
Dead Letter Office in Manhattan
(Yours, of course, the best)?

Yes, yes, it's just as expected,
Nervous Nellie, Willie the Weeper,
Each reluctant to speak up and say:
Look here, this is ridiculous!
Let's just embrace and part
The way they do in myths.

You be an old branch, perhaps
Ash, gnarled but with an ardent
Trace of fragrance. And I'll splash
Away across the bog, a river rat
With a cracked back foot.
We won't bother with farewells,

Both rendered speechless anyhow by
Transformation—just like my lucid,
Dazzling lost letters explaining
Everything, which even now the
Postmaster General is transcribing for
General distribution along Star Route,

Next to the Wanted posters on the wall
Where, fierce and separate, each of us looks out.

AFTER HOURS

Of course that's why I drink.
It hadn't dawned on me till now.
It took a madman and a very
dead poet and a local postman to
point out the obvious: I drink
because I no longer hear from you.

Of course that's why I can't sleep
or I sleep much of the day or take
cat-naps with a sleep-mask at noon.
What's more transparent? Naps and booze
and noon all scan and nearly rhyme
so I don't have to miss you all the time.

Of course that's why I rage
and shred bed clothes and weep
and pour pear brandy in a snifter,
scrambling downstairs at odd hours,
searching for my misplaced glove.
What would you have me do, love?

ALMOST AT LEISURE

Sometimes rough gin tastes
sweeter than his touch on your skin,
wild abandon on a worn blanket.

Sometimes you long for him to linger,
almost at leisure,
asking real questions
about the book lying open
on your bedside table
or the children.

FORECAST

I
JUST NOW

Something at once so crisp
And tender in the cluttered
Blend of Autumn splendor
Lends a contradiction to the day.

I bend to fondle the blond
Slender brush of tendrils
Just emerging at the root
Of sprouting shoots, without

Your dear attention. This
Escaping distance remains
Unassailable, something about
Your elusive face, all about

My alternate embrace of Fall,
Its annual evasion into frost.

II
THE POSTPONEMENT

Giddy Autumn is delayed this year,
Late as a kid called over and over
To the table. Supper's ready.
Everything is getting cold.
Get in here right this instant.

But she pays no attention,
Unconcerned with our demands.
So it stays warm all Fall, all
The leaves confused. No gaudy
Shawl of fuchsia stripes the land.

Just so your lack of absence baffles me,
Primed as I thought I was for Winter
And your loss. I mean I thought
The chill would happen faster.
Thanks for that bit of Summer in the air.

III
LEAVE-TAKING

Swans on the pond
And the slow rowing
Loosening bonds
And the not knowing
Autumn along
And the brief easing
Weather gone wrong
And the hard freezing.

EXIT

A little spillage in the grass.
Some cracks and shattering. Alas
For broken bottles, broken vows,
The bloody foot, the whys, the hows,
The explanation lightly tossed,
The crocus wilting in the frost.
The festered wound, the rage of leaving
Will heal without you. Enter grieving.

V

TIMES TWO

at a reading by Anne Carson

She was talking about the nature of desire
when you sat down beside me and I saw
your handsome face and thought, Well,
lucky me. When we began to speak about
everything, without restraint, I needed to recall
what makes for ecstasy is incompletion.

We each buy her latest book, signed
to each of us "respectfully." You observe
I am beaming. A drink seems just the thing.
At the Poetry Place next door, we discover
an unoccupied couch and settle in. You
buy me Scotch, yourself a glass of beer.
What could I give in return? A new poem
I'd thrust in the back pocket of my purse.
"The Postponement." Postponing. Just the thing.
I try to explain the poem. How loss takes place.
The colors things take on while fading.
The kindness of a certain kind of delay.

But what about desire, you inquire? To mention
the unmentionable is, of course, to mention it.
Carson was talking about Sappho, about how she is
preserved in fragments. Like an excavation.
Words carved on tablets lost on the Isle of Lesbos
eons ago. We each bring along our own history.
I need to leave for many reasons.

We walk together over the Embankment Bridge,
spangled with all the white lights of London.
Carson says ornament implies a kind of order.
Or is it chaos? We take the correction in stride,
striding towards the well-lit ancient station
where I'll take the tube away from you.
We open our arms and embrace.
I race down the metal staircase and find
the exact right train waiting to depart,
another kind of gift or deprivation.

THIS ABANDONED CHAPEL

I am considering the weathered beams of this stone chapel,
Built early in the last century. I am considering cobwebs
Glinting in the roving morning light, trees beyond the open
Arched window and the massive arched entrance to this place.

Six tall white candles dip and flare in the dim interior.
I have come here to light them for three people I know
Who died last week. Every week three people I know die.
Two others are for my parents, also dead. And one for you,
The only one alive among these burning tapers.

The flames rush and thrust ceilingward as though they
Didn't know, as though dead souls and living
Bear the same energy when flames come into play.

From the rafters, a twisted wire suspends a rusted lantern,
Its octagonal sides filigreed with dancing Cambodian maidens.
The floor, cement and fractured stone, is seamed with age.
Three carved benches face the makeshift altar,
An ancient table, empty of adornment. Nothing else
Here except for the candles, their glow consoling.

And when I blow them out, as I shall before leaving,
Will the dead souls shudder, feeling themselves flung
A little farther from the light?
Will you, far away and alive, feel a sudden breeze,
A chill about your throat, on your averted face?
That was my doing. Forgive me.
I would not quench your distant flame,
Even as this one candle gutters in your living name.

WHAT TO REMEMBER WHAT TO FORGET

in response to advice from a therapist

I

As though you have a choice,
Sweetmeats on display in a glass case:
Plump macaroons, a slice of lemon tart,
Three sour cherry bonbons, ginger chunks
To savor as you make your way back home.
These should last for at least a week
Of ruminations while you decide
What to keep and what discard from
All your bitter battles with the past.
Which among these delicacies
You'll wrap securely in wax paper,
Preserved for tasting on a better day?

II

I suck my candies with a grain of salt
Since wisdom emanates from mortal mouths,
From pros who make their living guiding lives.
And look how well things turned out for them.

STAGE THREE

A clown enters the room.
Hi Clown, says the small boy.
Sit down, Clown.
The clown sits down.

Behold! an upside-down
Clown, shouts the
Announcer. Lacks gravity.
Sit down, Clown.

He stands disguised as
A famous man. Wrapped
In his madness masquerade,
He struts and frets his
Way around the stove,
Boiling with rage, flushed
With grammatical detritus.
Noxious sentence fragments
Splatter the kitchen sink. He
Sinks to his chair
(Sit down, Clown),
Sobs in the breakfast nook,
Attired in his crimson
Academic robes. Go ahead.
Give him a hand. Three cheers
For your standard damaged
Heart survivor, chaos and repose.

GREETINGS

In guttering December
as the year hangs fire
ardent greetings arrive
from all the fair young men
who loved me once
except for the ones who are dead
but most of them are dead.

HOUSEKEEPING

The wise man says, Enough
Of these mortuary pieces,
Be done with them.
You have other fish to fry.
Live ones.
Aghast, the poet ponders, I do?

Love and death,
Declares the old adage,
The only two true subjects.
And when love's fled,
Well, here's the dead,
Staring you in the face.

Scientists have discovered
That rapturous happiness
Resides just a tiny bit
Back behind the ear,
Inside the complex cortex
Of the brain, whereas

Transient happiness lodges
Somewhat farther forward,
Shallow, like the forehead.
Grief, they say, is buried
Deep and shuts down
Completely if sadness persists

For weeks on end.
We might think of the brain
Like a house.
A massive mansion
With its fuses blown.
You live there, stumbling

About in the half light,
Bumping into loose
Electrical wires, broken
Back stairs, elusive paths
Leading through brambles.
There's a pond out back.
Maybe you even go
Fishing those murky waters.
A live one surfaces
Every time. Fry it gently.
It belongs to you. And
You are sad or happy,

Depending. So much for
Love and death all over again.
Welcome home.

DISSECTION STUDIES

But, finally even that ache is common & un-tragic...
—Kathleen Graber

The closest you can come to
knowledge of your heart's interstices:
a bulging plaster replica in Philadelphia
you pay good money to wander through
one afternoon, aorta into left auricle
leading into right ventricle into
chambers opening through tubes
propelling blood, murmuring heart
sounds—inaccurate enough, more
than enough to master or pretend
to know your own heart's pulsing,
fickle and relentlessly loyal, placed
beneath the cave of winds, between
the cage of ribs, the cliffs and
passageways defining boundaries
that daily keep you from meeting
head-on your heart.

ALMOST A PALLIATIVE

This is where the moon
takes over
its slick silver disc
a wound in the night sky
an open mouth
a cry or else
a circle of solace
a white gauze bandage
applied to an
open gash
that leaks in the night sky

see how, even as we speak,
it's beginning to turn red.

BATH AT EVENING

The consolation of water
permeates everything, not
entirely consoling but, more
often than not, warm.

Here an oval arc,
a knee, emerges
from the soapy surface
brimming in a claw-foot tub.

These pale familiar breasts,
two comfortable small
creatures, lounge at ease
on this naked chest.

My hand between my thighs
belongs right there.
Nothing is wrong
with glory in the woman.

All scant distraction
yields to water's gifts.
The ragings of the evening
evanesce—and I am here.

Ansie Baird holds degrees from Vassar College and the State University of New York at Buffalo, where she received her M.A. in English and won first prize in the University's Academy of American Poets contest. She is Poet in Residence and a part-time English teacher at The Buffalo Seminary, a non-sectarian secondary school in Buffalo, where she has taught for the past thirty-one years. She has also taught for Just Buffalo Literary Center in their Writers in Education program and was an original member of the Albright-Knox collaborative docent program entitled: A Picture's Worth A Thousand Words.

Her work has been published in The *Paris Review, Western Humanities Review, The Southern Review, The Denver Quarterly, Poetry Northwest, The South Dakota Review, The Quarterly, The Recorder, Earth's Daughters,* and a number of other journals.

Ansie Baird has conducted numerous poetry readings over the years in local and not so local venues. She is a life-long resident of Buffalo, New York.

THE WHITE PINE PRESS POETRY PRIZE